Why Do We Have Rules?

UNDERSTANDING CITIZENSHIP

Manuel Martinez

CIVICS FOR THE REAL WORLD™

Rosen Classroom™

There are many rules.

Do you know what they do?

Rules tell us how to act.

We say please and thank you.

Rules keep us safe.

We wait to cross the street.

Rules make games fair.
Everyone gets a turn.

Rules help us learn.
We raise our hands in class.

Why do we have rules?

Rules make the world better!

WORDS TO KNOW

game

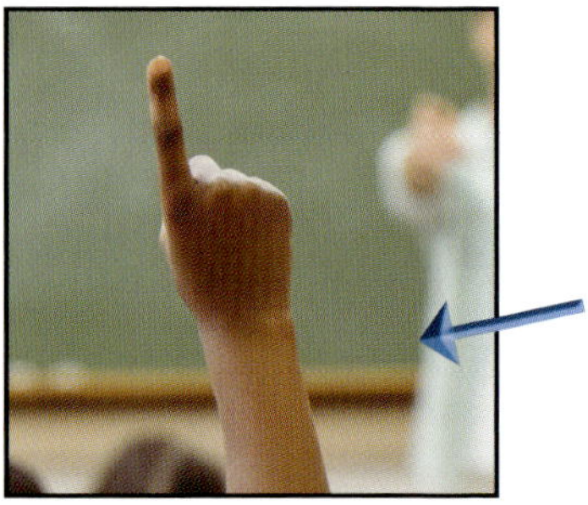

hand

street